Palette of Color
Monograph Series

The Chemistry of Natural Dyes

by Dianne N. Epp

Series Editor
Mickey Sarquis, Director
Center for Chemical Education

Terrific Science Press
Miami University Middletown
Middletown, Ohio

This monograph is intended for use by teachers, chemists, and properly supervised students. Teachers and other users must develop and follow procedures for the safe handling, use, and disposal of chemicals in accordance with local and state regulations and requirements. The cautions, warnings, and safety reminders associated with the doing of experiments and activities involving the use of chemicals and equipment contained in this publication have been compiled from sources believed to be reliable and to represent the best opinion on the subject as of 1995. However, no warranty, guarantee, or representation is made by the author, editor, or the Terrific Science Press as to the correctness or sufficiency of any information herein. Neither the author, editor, nor the publisher assumes any responsibility or liability for the use of the information herein, nor can it be assumed that all necessary warnings and precautionary measures are contained in this publication. Other or additional information or measures may be required or desirable because of particular or exceptional conditions or circumstances, or because of new or changed legislation.

Terrific Science Press
Miami University Middletown
4200 East University Blvd.
Middletown, Ohio 45042
513/727-3318

©1995 by Terrific Science Press
05   04   03   02   01   00   99   6   5   4   3   2

ISBN: 1-883822-06-8

This material is based upon work supported by the **National Science Foundation.** This project was supported, in part, by the National Science Foundation. Any opinions, findings, and conclusions or recommendations expressed in this material are those of the author and do not necessarily reflect the views of the National Science Foundation.

To my parents, who have always believed in me

and

To my Aunt Elma, who introduced me to natural dyes.

Contents

■ Acknowledgments

The author and editor wish to thank the following individuals who have contributed to the development of *The Chemistry of Natural Dyes.*

Terrific Science Press Design and Production Team
Susan Gertz, Amy Stander, Lisa Taylor, Thomas Nackid, Stephen Gentle, Anne Munson

Terrific Science Press Laboratory Testing Coordinator
Andrea Nolan

Reviewers
David H. Abrahams	Dexter Chemical Corporation	New York, NY
Susan Hershberger	Miami University	Oxford, OH
Linda Woodward	University of Southwestern Louisiana	Lafayette, LA

■ Foreword

The Chemistry of Natural Dyes is the second in a three-volume series of monographs entitled *Palette of Color.* This series is aimed at enabling high school chemistry teachers to introduce their students to a fascinating area of industrial chemistry—dyes and colorants. These monographs provide background information on the history and chemistry of various dyes and colorants, together with hands-on activities on producing, testing, and using these chemicals. Dianne Epp has brought together an excellent collection of chemistry activities in an easy-to-use format. As in all volumes published by Terrific Science Press, each of these activities has been tested by teachers in the Center for Chemical Education's (CCE) Terrific Science Programs and reviewed by experts in the field to ensure accuracy, safety, and pedagogical effectiveness. We believe that these monographs will enhance the relevance and appeal of the high school chemistry teacher's repertoire.

Dianne created these volumes while on a 1993–94 sabbatical from East High School in Lincoln, NE. During that year, Dianne joined the CCE team as a Teacher Fellow and worked on this and other curriculum-development efforts, including integrating microscale laboratory activities into Miami University's general chemistry curriculum. We want to thank Dianne for sharing her keen insights into the topics of dye chemistry, microscale chemistry, and chemical education; for her hard work in developing this series; and for allowing us to publish it.

In addition to the *Palette of Color* monograph series, the CCE offers many other science education opportunities and resource materials for teachers and students at all levels. These opportunities are outlined on Pages viii–xi. While each initiative within the Center has a unique focus and addresses the needs of a distinct population, all programs emphasize hands-on, inquiry-based chemical education through which students develop their abilities to work together to solve scientific challenges, think critically, and utilize their powers of observation.

We hope you will find that these monographs provide you with a useful and exciting way to involve your students in doing chemistry through integrated real-world themes. We welcome your comments at any time and are interested in learning about especially successful uses of these materials.

Mickey Sarquis, Director
Center for Chemical Education
May 1995

The Center for Chemical Education

Built on a tradition of quality programming, materials development, and networking between academia and industry, Miami University's Center for Chemical Education (CCE) encompasses a multifaceted collaboration of cross-grade-level and interdisciplinary initiatives begun in the mid-1980s as Terrific Science Programs. These initiatives are linked through the centrality of chemistry to the goal of fostering quality hands-on, minds-on science education for all students. CCE activities include credit coursework and other opportunities for educators at all levels; K–12 student programs; undergraduate, graduate, and postgraduate programs in chemical education; materials development, including teacher resource materials, program handbooks, and videos; and public outreach efforts and networking to foster new and existing partnerships among classroom teachers, university-based science educators, industrial scientists, and professional societies.

Professional Development for Educators

Credit Courses   The Center for Chemical Education offers a variety of summer and academic-year workshop-style courses for K–12 and college teachers. While each workshop has a unique focus, all reflect current pedagogical approaches in science education, cutting-edge academic and industrial research topics, and classroom applications for teachers and students. Short courses provide opportunities for educators to enrich their science teaching in a limited amount of time. All courses offer graduate credit.

Non-Credit Courses   Academies allow CCE graduates and other teachers to attend special one-day sessions presented by leading science educators from around the United States. Offerings include seminars, mini-workshops, and share-and-swap sessions.

Internships   Through 8- to 10-week summer internships, program graduates work as members of industrial teams to gain insight into the day-to-day workings of industrial laboratories, enabling them to bring real-world perspectives into the classroom.

Fellowships   Master teachers at primary, secondary, and college levels do research in chemical education and undertake curriculum and materials development as Teacher Fellows with the Center for Chemical Education. Fellowships are available for the summer and the academic year.

K–12 Student Programming

Summer Camps   A variety of summer camps are available to area elementary, middle, and high school students. These camps not only provide laboratory-based enrichment for students, but also enable educators in summer courses to apply their knowledge of hands-on exploration and leadership skills. Satellite camps are offered at affiliated sites throughout the country.

Science Carnivals   Carnivals challenge elementary school students with hands-on science in a non-traditional atmosphere, encouraging them to apply the scientific method to activities that demonstrate scientific principles. Sponsoring teachers and their students host these carnivals for other students in their districts.

Super Saturday Science Sessions	High school students are introduced to industrial and research applications of science and technology through special Saturday sessions that involve the students in experiment-based problem-solving. Topics have included waste management, environmental sampling, engineering technology, paper science, chemical analysis, microbiology, and many others.
Ambassador Program	Professional chemists, technicians, and engineers, practicing and recently retired, play important roles as classroom ambassadors for high school and two-year college students. Ambassadors not only serve as classroom resources, but they are also available as consultants when a laboratory scenario calls for outside expertise; they mentor special projects both in and out of the classroom; and they are available for career counseling and professional advice.

Undergraduate and Graduate Student Programming

Teaching Science with TOYS Undergraduate Course	This undergraduate course replicates the Teaching Science with TOYS teacher inservice program for the preservice audience. Students participate in hands-on physics and chemistry sessions.
General Chemistry Initiative	This effort is aimed at more effectively including chemical analysis and problem solving in the two-year college curriculum. To accomplish this goal, we are developing and testing discovery-based laboratory scenarios and take-home lecture supplements that illustrate topics in chemistry through activities beyond the classroom. In addition to demonstrating general chemistry concepts, these activities also involve students in critical-thinking and group problem-solving skills used by professional chemists in industry and academia.
Chemical Technology Curriculum Development	Curriculum and materials development efforts highlight the collaboration between college and high school faculty and industrial partners. These efforts will lead to the dissemination of a series of activity-based monographs, including detailed instructions for discovery-based investigations that challenge students to apply principles of chemical technology, chemical analysis, and Good Laboratory Practices in solving problems that confront practicing chemical technicians in the workplace.
Other Undergraduate Activities	The CCE has offered short courses/seminars for undergraduates that are similar in focus and pedagogy to CCE teacher/faculty enhancement programming. In addition, CCE staff members provide Miami University students with opportunities to interact in area schools through public outreach efforts and to undertake independent study projects in chemical education.
Degree Program	Miami's Department of Chemistry offers both a Ph.D. and M.S. in Chemical Education for graduate students who are interested in becoming teachers of chemistry in situations where a comprehensive knowledge of advanced chemical concepts is required and where acceptable scholarly activity can include the pursuit of chemical education research.

Educational Materials

The Terrific Science Press publications have emerged from CCE's work with classroom teachers of grades K–12 and college in graduate-credit, workshop-style inservice courses. Before being released, our materials undergo extensive classroom testing by teachers working with students at the targeted grade level, peer review by experts in the field for accuracy and safety, and editing by a staff of technical writers for clear, accurate, and consistent materials lists and procedures. For a complete listing of Terrific Science Press publications, visit our web site at:

www.terrificscience.org

Terrific Science Network

Affiliates College and district affiliates to CCE programs disseminate ideas and programming throughout the United States. Program affiliates offer support for local teachers, including workshops, resource/symposium sessions, and inservices; science camps; and college courses.

Industrial Partners We collaborate directly with over 40 industrial partners, all of whom are fully dedicated to enhancing the quality of science education for teachers and students in their communities and beyond.

Outreach On the average, graduates of CCE professional development programs report reaching about 40 other teachers through district inservices and other outreach efforts they undertake. Additionally, graduates, especially those in facilitator programs, institute their own local student programs. CCE staff also undertake significant outreach through collaboration with local schools, service organizations, professional societies, and museums.

Newsletters CCE newsletters provide a vehicle for network communication between program graduates, members of industry, and other individuals active in chemical and science education. Newsletters contain program information, hands-on science activities, teacher resources, and ideas on how to integrate hands-on science into the curriculum.

For more information about any of the CCE initiatives, contact us at:

Center for Chemical Education
4200 East University Blvd.
Middletown, OH 45042
513/727-3318
FAX: 513/727-3328
e-mail: *CCE@muohio.edu*
www.terrificscience.org

■ What Are the *Palette of Color* Monographs?

Look around you—color is everywhere. The clothes we wear, the food we eat, the posters with which we decorate our rooms; indeed all of our surroundings, natural and man-made, abound with color. From prehistoric times, people have been fascinated with color; from cave paintings to the latest computers, color has been our constant companion.

The *Palette of Color* monograph series enables high school chemistry teachers to challenge students to explore the chemistry behind dyes. Each monograph examines a different class of dyes and investigates the chemistry using principles common to most high school chemistry curricula. Hands-on, problem-solving activities involve students in answering questions posed about the dyes and their uses.

The Chemistry of Vat Dyes

Indigo and Inkodyes are used to illustrate how vat dyes are synthesized and used. Until the end of the 19th century, all colors were obtained from natural sources, but today the number of synthetic colorants exceeds 7,000. One class of these colorants, the vat dyes, contains not only the oldest natural dyes known, but also many important synthetic dyes. This class of dyes is studied in this monograph.

The Chemistry of Natural Dyes

For thousands of years, dyes were obtained from natural sources, such as plants and animals. Although synthetic dyes have replaced many natural dyes for commercial use, natural dyes still hold a fascination and are used extensively by artisans around the world. This monograph investigates the most common type of natural dyes, known as acid or anionic dyes, and their reactions with wool and eggshells.

The Chemistry of Food Dyes

Dyes aren't just for fabrics—colorants have been added to food for centuries to enhance its appearance. This monograph investigates both the compounds which give foods their natural color and the synthetic colorants currently approved for use in foods.

How to Use *The Chemistry of Natural Dyes*

The *Palette of Color* monographs are intended for use by a secondary chemistry teacher. A monograph may be inserted into the curriculum when the appropriate chemistry concept is being examined as a practical application of that concept. Monographs might also be used as independent study units for students.

Each monograph is organized in two parts: Teacher Background Information and Classroom Materials. The Teacher Background Information section includes a review of pertinent science content, notes and setups for the activities, and cross-curricular activities to supplement the science activities. The Classroom Materials section includes student background and activity handouts and overheads.

What's in *The Chemistry of Natural Dyes*

Until the end of the 19th century all colors were obtained from natural sources. Although synthetic dyes have replaced natural dyes for commercial use, natural dyes still hold a fascination and are used extensively by artisans around the world. This monograph investigates the most common type of natural dyes, known as acid or anionic dyes, and their reactions with wool and eggshells.

What Students Do

In this monograph, students do the following:

- experiment with a traditional method of dyeing eggs, using natural materials as the source of the dyes;
- study the chemistry of natural acid dyes as they interact with protein fibers, using wool as an example;
- examine the pH-dependency of several natural dyes;
- experiment with several different mordants and observe their effects on dye colors; and
- devise a method to test dyed samples for colorfastness.

Key Ideas

The following key ideas are covered:

- acid-base chemistry of natural dyes;
- metallic mordants as an example of complex ion chemistry; and
- examination of industrial testing procedures.

Time Frame

Teachers should select from the variety of activities to fit the time available. A minimum of three 50-minute lessons would be needed to cover the topic of natural dyes.

■ Employing Appropriate Safety Procedures

Experiments, demonstrations, and hands-on activities add relevance, fun, and excitement to science education at any level. However, even the simplest activity can become dangerous when the proper safety precautions are ignored or when the activity is done incorrectly or performed by students without proper supervision. While the activities in this book include cautions, warnings, and safety reminders from sources believed to be reliable and while the text has been extensively reviewed by classroom teachers and university scientists, it is your responsibility to develop and follow procedures for the safe execution of the activities you choose to do. You are also responsible for the safe handling, use, and disposal of chemicals in accordance with local and state regulations and requirements.

Safety First

- Collect and read the Materials Safety Data Sheets (MSDS) for all of the chemicals used in your experiments. MSDS's provide physical property data, toxicity information, and handling and disposal specifications for chemicals. They can be obtained upon request from manufacturers and distributors of these chemicals. In fact, MSDS's are often shipped with chemicals when they are ordered. These should be collected and made available to students, faculty, or parents for information about specific chemicals used in these activities.

- Read and follow the American Chemical Society Minimum Safety Guidelines for Chemical Demonstrations on the next page. Remember that you are a role model for your students—your attention to safety will help them develop good safety habits while assuring that everyone has fun with these activities.

- Read each activity carefully and observe all safety precautions and disposal procedures. Determine and follow all local and state regulations and requirements.

- Never attempt an activity if you are unfamiliar or uncomfortable with the procedures or materials involved. Consult a college or industrial chemist for advice or ask him or her to perform the activity for your class. These people are often delighted to help.

- Always practice activities yourself before using them with your class. This is the only way to become thoroughly familiar with an activity, and familiarity will help prevent potentially hazardous (or merely embarrassing) mishaps. In addition, you may find variations that will make the activity more meaningful to your students.

- You, your assistants, and any students participating in the preparation for or doing of the activity must wear safety goggles if indicated in the activity and at any other time you deem necessary.

- Special safety instructions are not given for everyday classroom materials being used in a typical manner. Use common sense when working with hot, sharp, or breakable objects. Keep tables or desks covered to avoid stains. Keep spills cleaned up to avoid falls.

ACS Minimum Safety Guidelines for Chemical Demonstrations

This section outlines safety procedures that Chemical Demonstrators must follow at all times.

1. Know the properties of the chemicals and the chemical reactions involved in all demonstrations presented.

2. Comply with all local rules and regulations.

3. Wear appropriate eye protection for all chemical demonstrations.

4. Warn the members of the audience to cover their ears whenever a loud noise is anticipated.

5. Plan the demonstration so that harmful quantities of noxious gases (e.g., NO_2, SO_2, H_2S) do not enter the local air supply.

6. Provide safety shield protection wherever there is the slightest possibility that a container, its fragments, or its contents could be propelled with sufficient force to cause personal injury.

7. Arrange to have a fire extinguisher at hand whenever the slightest possibility for fire exists.

8. Do not taste or encourage spectators to taste any non-food substance.

9. Never use demonstrations in which parts of the human body are placed in danger (such as placing dry ice in the mouth or dipping hands into liquid nitrogen).

10. Do not use "open" containers of volatile, toxic substances (e.g., benzene, CCl_4, CS_2, formaldehyde) without adequate ventilation as provided by fume hoods.

11. Provide written procedure, hazard, and disposal information for each demonstration whenever the audience is encouraged to repeat the demonstration.

12. Arrange for appropriate waste containers for and subsequent disposal of materials harmful to the environment.

Part A: Teacher Background Information

What Are Natural Dyes?
What Is a Dye?

Classifying Dyes

The Structure of Wool

Dyeing Wool

Notes and Setups for Activities
Activity 1: Sassy Eggs

Activity 2: What Color Will Appear?

Activity 3: How Is Dye Color pH-Dependent?

Activity 4: How Do Mordants Affect Dye Colors?

Activity 5: How Colorfast Are Natural Dyes?

Extensions

Supplementary Activities and Information
Literature Integration

Other Cross-Curricular Integration

Dye Terms and Common Language Expressions

References

What Are Natural Dyes?

What Is a Dye?

Colorants for textiles include dyes and pigments. Dyes are organic chemicals which selectively absorb and reflect wavelengths of light within the visible spectrum. Dyes usually diffuse into the interior of a fiber from a water solution. Pigments are water-insoluble, microscopic-sized color particles that are usually held to the surface of a fiber by a resin. In this monograph we will limit our investigation to the use of dyes as colorants for textiles.

Dye molecules vary greatly in composition and behavior. A typical dye molecule contains at least three unique chemical groups, each responsible for a particular property of the dye. The chromophore is the color-producing portion of the dye molecule, and the auxochrome influences the intensity of the dye and provides a site at which the dye can chemically bond to the fabric. These chemical groups include the typical examples shown in Figure A1. The solubilizing group allows the dye molecule to be water soluble so that it is capable of interacting with a fiber in a water bath.

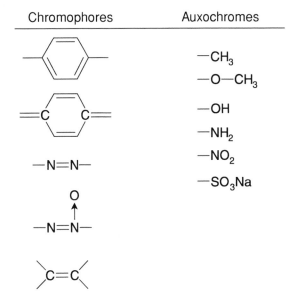

Figure A1: Typical chemical groups of dye molecules

Classifying Dyes

Dyes may be classified in a number of ways, including the chemical constitution of the dye and its method of application to the fabric. In a dye bath, the dye molecule must be in a water-soluble form. It may exist as neutral molecules or it may ionize and the dye fragment may be the cation (+ charged) or the anion (– charged).

The majority of natural dyes occur as anionic dyes, also known as acid dyes because they are best used in a bath which is slightly acidic. The dye fragment in acid dyes is negatively charged (an anion), and it will form a strongly ionic bond with a fiber which has a cationic (+ charged) bonding site. In this monograph, we limit our discussion to the chemistry of acid dyes as they react with wool.

The Structure of Wool

Wool is made up of a protein called keratin. As is typical with proteins, the average molecular weight (molar mass) of keratin is approximately 60,000. Keratin is a complex polypeptide polymer made from 18 different types of amino acids. (See Figure A2.) The sequence of these amino acid residues is known as the primary structure of the protein.

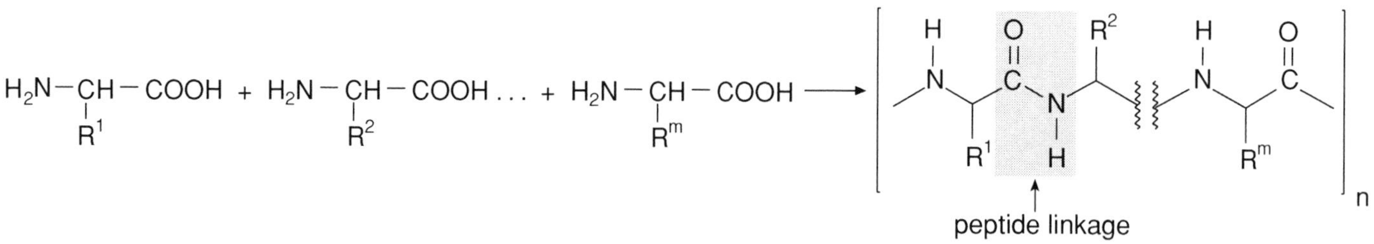

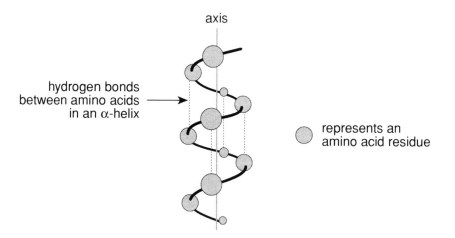

Figure A2: Polymerization of amino acids to form keratin. R^1 to R^m represent the side chains of different types of amino acids that make up the primary structure of this protein. A peptide bond that joins the two amino acid residues is highlighted.

The primary structure is usually represented with the atoms written in a line, as in Figure A2. On paper, Figure A2 appears flat, or two-dimensional. However, the polypeptide forms a three-dimensional secondary structure.

The secondary structure (the regular repetitive pattern that gives the protein chain its basic backbone shape) of the keratin protein chains is held by intramolecular hydrogen bonding in an alpha-helix (α-helix) orientation. (See Figure A3.) Alpha-helixes follow the path of a right-handed spiral. This means that the α-helix always has a right-handed direction, so that if the thumb of your right hand points along the axis of the helix, your fingers curl in the same direction as the curl of the spiral.

axis

hydrogen bonds between amino acids in an α-helix

represents an amino acid residue

Figure A3: Intramolecular hydrogen bonding holds the keratin in an α-helix orientation.

The helical structure of keratin is caused by intramolecular hydrogen bonding within the protein chain. The amine N–H group of each amino acid residue in the chain forms a hydrogen bond with the carbonyl oxygen four amino acid residues further along the polypeptide chain.

In wool and other fibrous proteins like hair, several α-helical polypeptide chains intertwine in a parallel, side-by-side fashion to form long, multichain superhelix cables called protofibrils. There are four types of interactions that hold these chains together: intermolecular hydrogen bonds, ionic bonds, disulfide bridge bonds, and hydrophobic interactions. Figure A4 provides a simplified overview of these four types of interchain interactions.

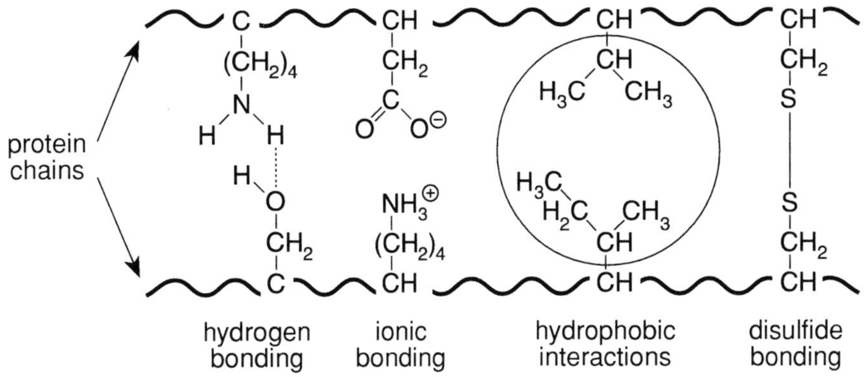

Figure A4: Four types of forces are typically responsible for holding the protein molecules in keratin together.

The disulfide bonds provide the only covalent bonds between adjoining α-helixes and are formed when two cysteine units (whether on the same chain or on two different chains) are oxidized to form a single cystine unit. (See Figure A5.) In addition to adding strength to the fiber, the pattern of disulfide bonds influences and fixes the curliness of the fiber.

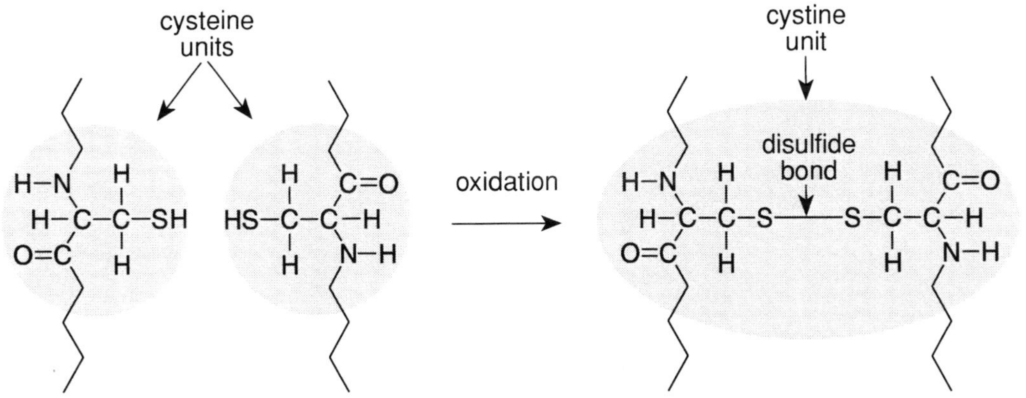

Figure A5: A disulfide bond is formed between two cysteine units.

Protofibrils are bundled together into microfibrils which are in turn bundled into macrofibrils to provide much of the strength we associate with natural fibers. (See Figure A6.) The springiness of wool fiber (and hair) results from the tendency of the α-helical cables to untwist when stretched and spring back when the external force is removed. Moderate stretching of the fibers involves breaking the hydrogen bonds, but not the stronger covalent bonds. Releasing the stretch typically allows the fiber to return to its original shape as the hydrogen bonds are re-formed.

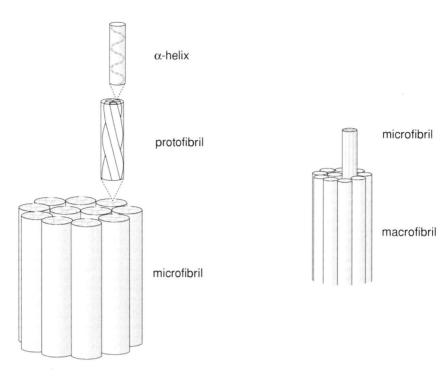

Figure A6: Alpha-helixes in fibrous proteins aggregate to form protofibrils, which are in turn bundled together into microfibrils and then macrofibrils.

Dyeing Wool

Acid dyes are dyes which contain an acid functional group such as $-SO_3H$ or $-COOH$. These dyes ionize in water, yielding dye fragments which are negatively charged ions. (See Figure A7.)

$$\text{dye}-(SO_3H)_n \ + \ H_2O \ \longrightarrow \ \text{dye}-(SO_3^{\ominus})_n \ + \ H_3O^{\oplus}$$

Figure A7: An acid dye is ionized in water.

When using an acid dye, the negatively charged dye fragment is attracted to the cationic site in the keratin, forming an ionic bond with the fiber. (See Figure A8.)

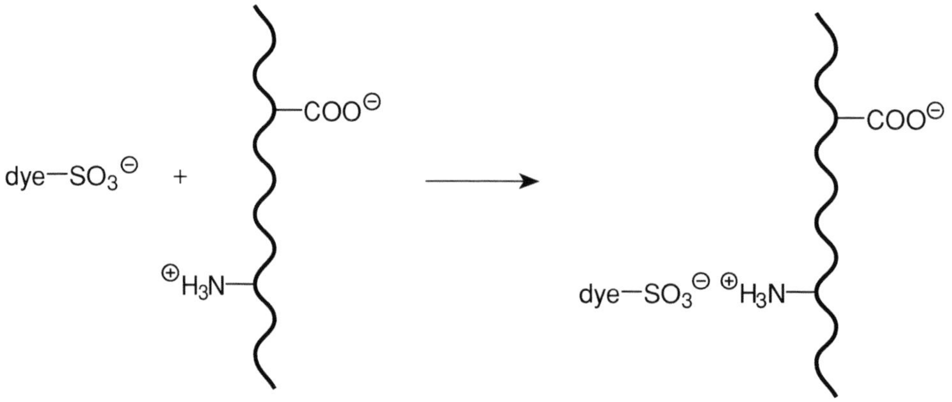

Figure A8: Reaction of an acid dye with keratin

If the acidity of the dye bath is increased, a larger number of amino groups in the keratin will be protonated; thus the pH of the dye bath has a direct affect on the ability of keratin to accept anionic dyes. Severe changes in pH can completely disrupt the structure of, or denature, keratin. Denaturation might be compared to stretching a spring out of shape, causing the neat coils to become a tangled mass of metal. In the case of a denatured protein, one is left with a long-chain polymer which has lost its important characteristics. When a protein is exposed to extreme changes in acidity, the hydrogen bonds that hold the helical structure in place and the salt bridges and disulfide bonds that hold the coils in specific layers or fibers are disrupted, causing irreversible denaturation.

However, increasing the dye bath acidity can also protonate the $-SO_3^-$ groups, changing the dye in the dye bath (the reverse of the reaction shown in Figure A7). Instead of using acid to change the receptivity of the fiber to the dye, other cations (often metal ions) can be employed. These metal cations are called mordants.

Mordants are used in the dyeing process to provide a bridge between the dye molecules and the fiber. Aluminum, tin, iron, copper, and chromium are metal ions commonly used as mordants. The hydrogen bonds in the keratin provide the site of attachment for the mordant metal ions. Metals that are used as mordants must be able to act as electron acceptors to form coordinate covalent bonds. The metal ion can then act as a bridge between the dye molecule and the fiber, often through oxygen from the $-OH$ or $-SO_3^-$ groups. Figure A9 provides a generalization for this process.

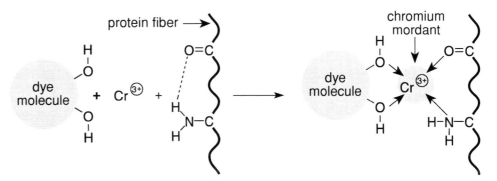

Figure A9: Generalized representation of the chromium mordant ion providing a link between the dye molecule and the protein fiber

Natural dyes that were important mordant dyes were often dihydroxy anthraquinones, such as alizarin (See Figure A10), which is the red coloring material in the madder family of plants. Aluminum ions and calcium ions were used as mordants for alizarin to provide the famous Turkey red color.

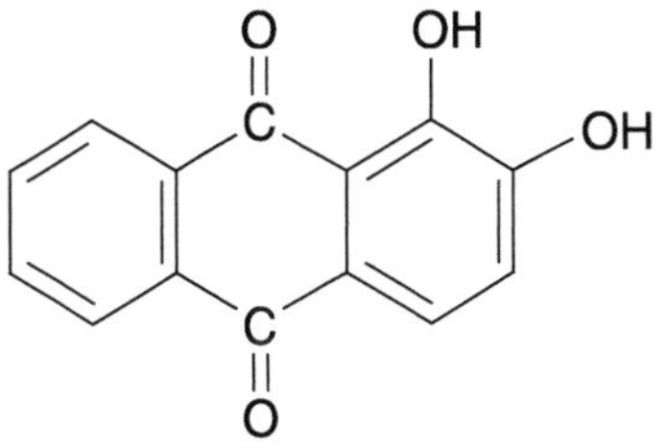

Figure A10: Structure of alizarin

Mordants react with dye molecules to form large, insoluble complexes sometimes known as "lakes." Mordants increase the fastness of the dye since the large complex cannot easily migrate out of the fiber.

Other important natural dyes were cochineal, a dyestuff made from the dried bodies of female cochineal insects (The color component is carminic acid), with tin ion as a mordant to produce a scarlet dye and logwood (The color component is haematin) with a chromium ion mordant to produce a rare black. (See Figure A11.)

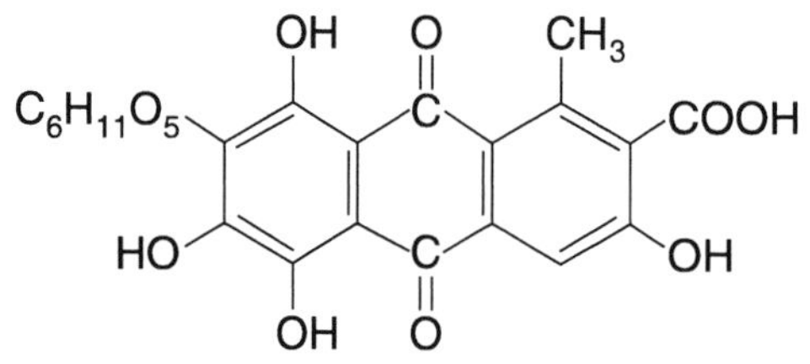

carminic acid
(cochineal)

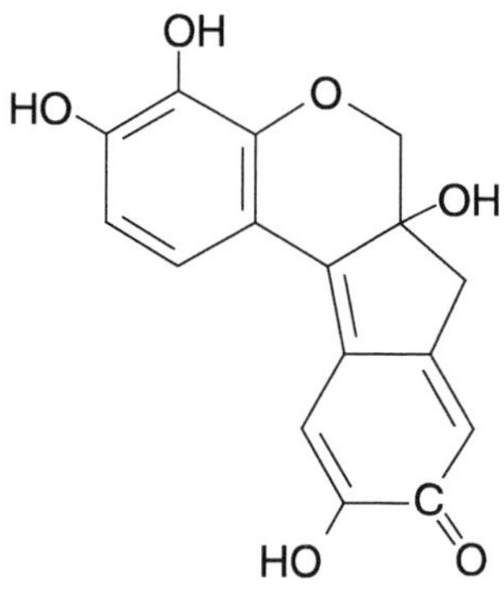

haematin
(logwood)

Figure A11: Color components of cochineal and logwood

■ Notes and Setups for Activities

Activity 1: Sassy Eggs

Students are introduced to the application of plant materials as natural dyes as they dye eggshells using onion skins and coffee. (See the photograph of Sassy Eggs on the cover.) Until the second half of the 19th century, virtually all egg dyeing was done with natural dyes.

Safety and Disposal

While many plants will provide natural dyes, they are not all edible. Because eggshells are porous, some of the dyes may penetrate the shell and contaminate the egg inside. While the dyes from onion skins and coffee are nontoxic, the leaves, flowers, and any potential residue in the beaker may be of questionable or unknown toxicity. As a result, eggs should not be consumed. Alternatively, the eggshells can be blown out.

Materials

Per student
*   blown-out eggshell or hard-boiled egg

To prepare the blown-out eggshell, use a large needle to break a small hole in each end of a clean, raw egg. Blow into one hole to force the contents out of the egg into a dish. Rinse and dry the eggshell.

*   outer skins of 2–3 medium-sized yellow onions
*   variety of small flowers or leaves
*   piece of white cotton cloth (about 20 cm x 20 cm)
*   rubber band
*   400-mL beaker
*   2–3 heaping spoonsful of fresh coffee grounds
*   tongs
*   hot plate (can be shared by several students)
*   (optional) a few drops of vegetable oil
*   (optional) a small beaker, such as a 50-mL beaker

Activity 2: What Color Will Appear?

Students extract the dye colors from natural materials and use them to dye pieces of wool. Wool yarn can be purchased from most shops that sell knitting supplies or ordered from Quinnehticut Woolen Co., P.O. Box 522, Norwich, CT 06360. Natural, unbleached yarn is preferable for dyeing as residual bleach may affect the colors. Help the students understand that not every dyed sample of a material will be the same color when using natural dyes. No two plants are identical in composition due to growing conditions and impurities. It is this very uniqueness which makes natural dyes fascinating. Distilled water or soft water must always be used when dyeing as the minerals in hard water will interfere with the dye process.

Safety and Disposal

Eye protection should be worn for this experiment.

Materials

Per pair of students
- 6 250-mL beakers
- 400-mL beaker
- glass stirring rod
- beaker tongs
- 4 pieces of wool yarn each approximately 10 cm long
- hot plate
- green tops from 3 or 4 carrots
- yellow onion skins (about 150 mL dry)
- distilled water
- 4 zipper-type plastic bags
- masking tape and pen for labels
- 3 Red Zinger® Tea bags
- 4 chamomile tea bags

Red Zinger is an herbal tea marketed by Celestial Seasonings, Boulder, CO. Its dye ingredient is hibiscus flowers. Other herbal teas containing hibiscus may be substituted. Pure chamomile tea is marketed by R.C. Bigelow Inc., Fairfield, CT 06430.

- goggles for each student

Results

Typical Results for Activity 2	
Dye Material	Color
onion skins	tan
carrot tops	light cream
Red Zinger	peach
chamomile	light cream

Answers to Summary Questions

1. No. The green carrot tops produced a yellowish dye bath and the deep red of the Red Zinger came from only slightly reddish material.

2. No. The Red Zinger was a very deep red dye bath but gave only a light peach color to the yarn. The greenish chamomile gave a light cream color to the yarn.

3. The onion skins appear to provide the strongest dye material.

4. The Red Zinger sample was quite red when removed from the dye bath, but after washing, very little of the color remained on the yarn.

Activity 3: How Is Dye Color pH-Dependent?

Students investigate how changing pH affects the color of two natural dyes on wool yarn. Since wool has both cationic and anionic sites, $-NH_3^+$ and $-COO^-$, both acid and base dyes can be used to dye wool. Most natural dyes are anionic (– charged) or acid dyes so the change of pH especially affects the dye because of the increase or decrease of $-NH_3^+$ sites.

Safety and Disposal

Eye protection should be worn for this experiment; ammonia and its vapors can damage the eyes. Do not wear contact lenses when working with ammonia because gaseous vapors may condense on the contact lens and damage the eye. Use ammonia only in a well-ventilated area. Should contact with the eyes occur, rinse the affected area with water for 15 minutes and seek medical attention while rinsing is occurring.

Materials

Per pair of students
- 3 250-mL beakers
- 6 150-mL beakers
- glass stirring rod
- beaker tongs
- 4 Hydrion paper strips
- 6 pieces of wool yarn each approximately 10 cm long
- 6 zipper-type plastic bags
- green tops from 3 to 4 carrots
- yellow onion skins (about 150 mL dry)
- about 3 mL vinegar
- about 3 mL 1 M ammonia solution
- hot plate
- distilled water
- goggles for each student

Getting Ready

A solution of 1 M ammonia, NH_3 (aq), can be purchased or prepared according to this ratio: 1 mL concentrated (15 M) NH_3 (aq) per 15 mL final volume. For example, to prepare 45 mL 1 M ammonia (enough for a typical class to do the activity), dissolve 3 mL concentrated (15 M) ammonia with water to a final volume of 45 mL. Because splattering may occur in this mixing process, it is recommended that the 3 mL 15 M NH_3 (aq) be slowly added to about 40 mL water; once mixed, the final volume can be adjusted to the desired 45-mL level with additional water.

Results

Colors will vary from dye bath to dye bath. The following are given as one set of typical data.

Typical Data for Activity 3			
Beaker Number	Dye Material	pH	Color
1	carrot tops	3–4	yellow-green
2	carrot tops	6–7	cream
3	carrot tops	10	blue-green
1	onion skins	3–4	orange
2	onion skins	6–7	bronze
3	onion skins	10	yellow

Answers to Summary Questions

1. Wool is attacked by strong bases at the disulfide bonds; therefore, a strong base will break down the structure of the cross-linking that holds the polymer together.

2. The basic soap solution would neutralize the protonated sites in the wool and would wash out the dye.

Activity 4: How Do Mordants Affect Dye Colors?

Students observe the effect of several metal ions as mordants for different natural dyes. Students should become aware that different mordants will have different effects on the same dye.

Because of the number of beakers and hot plates required, it is a good idea to group four students together. Two students can prepare the mordant baths and two students can prepare the dye baths.

Safety and Disposal

Eye protection should be worn for this experiment.

Materials

Per group of 4 students
- 4 250-mL beakers
- 4 100-mL beakers
- 2 glass stirring rods
- 16 pieces of wool yarn (each about 10 cm long)

- 2 hot plates
- beaker tongs
- yellow onion skins (about 150 mL dry)
- green tops from 3–4 carrots
- 3 Red Zinger tea bags
- 4 chamomile tea bags
- 1.5 g copper sulfate pentahydrate ($CuSO_4 \cdot 5H_2O$)
- 1.5 g alum, $AlNH_4(SO_4)_2$ or $KAl(SO_4)_2$
- 2.75 g cream of tartar
- 0.35 g tin(II) chloride ($SnCl_2$)
- distilled water
- goggles for each student

Results

Colors will vary for each dye bath. The following are given as one set of typical data.

Typical Results for Activity 4		
Dye Material	Mordant	Color
carrot tops	copper	green
	alum	light yellow-green
	tin	deep yellow
	no mordant	light cream
onion skins	copper	brown
	alum	bronze
	tin	orange
	no mordant	tan
Red Zinger	copper	brown
	alum	peach
	tin	dark green-black
	no mordant	peach
chamomile	copper	yellow-green
	alum	yellow
	tin	deep bronze yellow
	no mordant	light cream

Answers to Summary Questions

1. No, each dye seemed to have different reactions to the mordants. One could not predict what color would result.

2. In the cases studied, the tin appeared to effect the most dramatic changes.

3. The wool mordanted with tin tended to feel stiff and somewhat brittle. Even though it causes dramatic color changes, tin would not appear to be a good mordant for wool as it affects the quality of the wool.

4. The alum seemed to cause the least change.

Activity 5: How Colorfast Are Natural Dyes?

Students set up protocols for testing procedures much as are used in an industrial setting. Textile colors are commonly tested for colorfastness (also known as light fastness). Early manufacturers used sunlight as the light source, but variation in duration and intensity from day to day made standardization difficult. On the other hand, many artificial light sources are unsuitable since they do not emit the same spectral range as sunlight. Xenon arc lamps with filters are often used in artificial testing, as their output corresponds quite closely to that of sunlight. Some companies, however, still prefer testing for light fastness in direct sunlight.

In this experiment students plan a procedure for testing their samples in sunlight, allowing for an ample exposure time. At a minimum, three weeks will probably be needed to observe any significant color changes.

Safety and Disposal

No special safety or disposal procedures are required.

Materials

Per group of 4 students
- sheet of uncorrugated cardboard (The back of a tablet will work well.)
- duct tape or black plastic tape
- transparent tape
- yarn samples from Activity 4

Answers to Summary Questions

1. Answers will vary.

2. Answers will vary.

3. Generally, mordanted dyes were significantly more colorfast than unmordanted dyes.

Extensions

The activities in this monograph are very open-ended. Students may be interested in trying to extract dyes from a variety of plants. Other herbal teas, flowers of various kinds, and some other vegetable material might be investigated.

Students can experiment with other metallic salts (including iron(III) nitrate, sodium chloride, and sodium bicarbonate) as mordants.

Students can devise various other methods of colorfastness testing, and they may be interested in testing the dyes for wash-fastness as well.

■ Supplementary Activities and Information

Literature Integration

Have students research and report on the importance of colored eggs in the mythology and folk customs of countries around the world.

Have students compile a list of literary quotations related to colors using *The Oxford English Dictionary* (R.W. Burchfield, Library of Congress, Washington, DC, 1988) or *The Home Book of Quotations* (B. Stevenson, Greenwich House, New York, 1984, ISBN 0517431300).

Have students read and discuss, "Words to a Young Weaver," by Noël Bennett (text provided).

Words to a Young Weaver

Noël Bennett

We are the Dineh,* my child,
With the Earth we live
With the Sky we live
   With the plants we live
   We know their ways.

Heed well the plants, my child.
Learn the ways of each, my child.
Some you must ask for gently,
   Pick their tips
   Heat them softly
   And they give.

Some you must demand of strongly
   Dig through the rock
   Pound hard the roots
   You will tire
   And they will give.
Give to each as it requires
It will give to you, my child,
It will give to you.

We are the Dineh,
With the Earth we live
With the Sky we live
   With the Plants we live
   We know their ways.

*Navajo word for themselves meaning "the people."

Nature comes as it comes
    Gives as it gives.
We do not plan Nature.
We do not control Nature.
    It is so in dyeing the wool.

Receive your colors as they come.
Learn the ways of each.
Some plants dye strong enough alone.
Some take strength from other things.
    The Ashes of the Juniper
    The Minerals of the Soil
Give to the weak, strength, my child
    And the colors that come are good.

The Red of the cliffs at sunset, will come.
The Yellow of the shimmering sand, will come.
The Green of the plant life around, will come.
The Black of the thunderclouds heavy will come.
All good colors will come, my child.
All good colors will come.

And do not try to match a color of the past.
    This is a new day.
    This is a new plant.
The colors that come forth are many,
None will be the same
And each that comes is good
And each that comes is good.

Source: Natural Plant Dyeing, *Brooklyn Botanic Garden, Brooklyn, NY, 1973.*

Other Cross-Curricular Integration

The following activities are suggestions for integrating the scientific study of natural dyes with other disciplines.

History and Economics

Have students research and report on one of the following topics: the history of the dye industry; how the exploration of the new world affected the dye industry through the discovery of new dye materials; or the powerful guild system and its attempts to create protectionist policies such as bans on the importation of certain dye materials.

Art

Much information is available on the art of home dyeing. Students could carry out major dyeing projects to color old wool sweaters or socks. Alternatively, they may dye a larger amount of yarn and create an article of apparel or a piece of fiber art.

Have students investigate how the American Indians of the Southwest United States used natural dyes in their weaving.

Biology/Botany

Have students research and report on the botanical families of dye-bearing plants.

Dye Terms and Common Language Expressions

Brazil This name came from the great forests of red-wooded trees that covered the northern part of the South American continent. Early European traders in the region gave it the name "Terra de Brazil" from the Portuguese word, *brasa,* meaning "live coals," a reference to the color of the wood. The wood of these trees, now known as brazilwood trees, yields red and purple dyes.

Britain This is the oldest name for England. It is a Latinized form of "Brythen," a Celtic word meaning "painted men." When Julius Caesar's army invaded England they found the Celts who lived there painted their bodies with extract of the woad plant.

Dyed in the Wool This phrase describes fleece dyed before it has been spun, thus fleece dyed of one color throughout. Today this phrase describes one who adheres strongly to a belief or tradition and is not likely to change.

Navy Blue King George II chose indigo to dye cloth for the British naval uniform, thus giving rise to the term "navy blue."

Off-Color This is a dyer's term meaning a color which was not true or deviated from the standard. Thus an "off-color" joke is one deemed unacceptable because it deviates from the standard morality.

Red Tape This phrase has become synonymous with legal or bureaucratic paperwork. The safflower was cultivated in Europe for the clear pinkish-red color it imparted to cotton and silk. The most important use of this dye was in coloring cotton tapes used to tie together legal documents—the original "red tape" so familiar to bureaucrats.

Royal Purple Purple is used to denote wealth or position. Tyrian purple was a dye extracted from mollusk shells abundant near Tyre on the shores of the Mediterranean Sea. This dye was exceedingly expensive because 12,000 shells were needed to obtain 1.4 g of the dye. During the Roman era, emperors, kings and priests paid the equivalent of $300/kg for wool dyed with Tyrian purple. "Born to the purple," came to mean "royal." Victor Hugo in *The Vanishing City* wrote, "The despot's wickedness comes of ill teaching and of power's excesses, comes of the purple he in childhood wears."

True Blue This phrase refers to a constant or loyal person. In dyer's terminology, a color which was fast and did not fade was known as "true" and blue was an especially difficult color to make fast. Hence, the phrase describes a valuable quality—constancy in a dye or in a person.

■ References

Adrosko, R.J. *Natural Dyes and Home Dyeing;* Dover: New York, 1971.

Casselman, K.L. *Craft of the Dyer;* University of Toronto: Toronto, Canada, 1980.

Coskey, E. *Easter Eggs for Everyone;* Abingdon: Nashville, TN, 1973.

Gordon, P.F.; Gregory, P. *Organic Chemistry of Color;* Springer-Verlag: New York, 1983.

Hatch, K.L. *Textile Science;* West: St. Paul, MN, 1993.

Leggett, W.F. *Ancient and Medieval Dyes;* Chemical Publishing: Brooklyn, NY, 1944.

McRae, B. *Colors From Nature;* Storey: Pownal, VT, 1993.

Natural Plant Dyeing; Weigle, P., Ed.; Brooklyn Botanic Gardens: New York, 1973.

Needles, H.L. *Fibers, Dyes, Finishes and Processes;* Noyes: Park Ridge, NJ, 1986.

Niles, J.N. *The Art and Craft of Natural Dyeing;* University of Tennessee: Knoxville, TN, 1990.

Storey, J. *Dyes and Fabrics;* Thames and Hudson: London, 1978.

Trotman, E.R. *Dyeing and Chemical Technology of Textile Fibers,* 6th ed.; Charles Griffin: High Wycomb, England, 1984.

Weigle, P. *Ancient Dyes for Modern Weavers;* Watson-Guptill: New York, 1974.

Wood, C.G. "Natural Dyes," *Chem Matters.* 1986, 4(4), 4–8.

Part B: Classroom Materials

What's Sassy About Sassy Eggs?

    Activity 1: Sassy Eggs

    Student Background 1: The Historical Importance of Natural Dyes

    Overhead 1: The Dye Works

What Makes Dyes Work?

    Student Background 2: Natural Dyes and Wool

    Overhead 2: Hydrogen Bonding in Keratin

    Overhead 3: Four Types of Interactions or Forces in Keratin

    Overhead 4: Formation of a Cystine Unit from the Oxidation of Two Cysteine Units

What's Your Favorite Color?

    Student Background 3: Natural Sources of Important Colors

    Overhead 5: A Madder Plant

    Activity 2: What Color Will Appear?

Can We Change a Dye's Color?

    Activity 3: How Is Dye Color pH-Dependent?

    Overhead 6: Ionic bonding Between Anionic Dye and Cationic Site on the Protein Fiber

    Student Background 4: Mordants

    Activity 4: How Do Mordants Affect Dye Colors?

    Overhead 7: The Mordant Chromium Ion Provides a Link Between the Dye Molecule and the Protein Fiber

Will the Dye Color Fade?

    Student Background 5: Fast or Fugitive?

    Activity 5: How Colorfast Are Natural Dyes?

What's Sassy About Sassy Eggs?

Activity 1: Sassy Eggs

The egg is one of the oldest symbols in recorded history. In many cultures, the egg is considered the symbol of the rebirth of the Earth out of the bleakness of winter. In such varied places as Egypt, Finland, and Hawaii, myths of the creation of the universe center around the world appearing out of an egg.

The giving and receiving of colored eggs is part of traditions in many parts of the world. Until the second half of the 19th century, virtually all egg dyeing was done with natural dyes obtained from plant material. Still widely used for egg dyeing in some parts of Europe, natural dyes produce softer shades than commercial synthetic dyes.

In the eastern part of the Netherlands, many customs are of ancient Saxon origin. People refer to these customs as Sassy. Even today, Sassy decorated eggs are made by Dutch people living in the eastern part of the Netherlands.

Safety

While many plants will provide natural dyes, they are not all edible. Because eggshells are porous, some of the dyes may penetrate the shell and contaminate the egg inside. While the dyes from onion skins and coffee are nontoxic, the leaves, flowers, and any potential residue in the beaker may be of questionable or unknown toxicity. As a result, eggs should not be consumed. Alternatively, the eggshells can be blown out.

Materials

Per student
- blown-out eggshell or hard-boiled egg
- outer skins of 2–3 medium-sized yellow onions
- variety of small flowers or leaves
- piece of white cotton cloth (about 20 cm x 20 cm)
- rubber band
- 400-mL beaker
- 2–3 heaping spoonsful of fresh coffee grounds
- tongs
- hot plate (can be shared by several students)
- (optional) a few drops of vegetable oil
- (optional) a small beaker, such as a 50-mL beaker

Procedure

1. Place the square of cloth on the table and cover it with a layer of onion skins.

2. Arrange leaves and flowers on top of the onion skins.

3. Place the hard-boiled egg or blown-out eggshell in the middle of the cloth and gather the cloth around it by the four corners. (See Figure B1.) Cover the egg so that it is completely surrounded by the onion skins, leaves, and flowers.

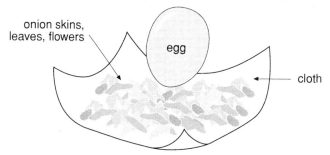

Figure B1: Covering the egg with onion skins, leaves and flowers, and cloth

4. Use a rubber band to fix the cloth snugly to the egg so that the bundle will stay together. (See Figure B2.)

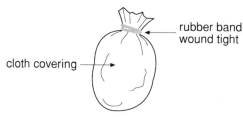

Figure B2: Securing the bundle with a rubber band

5. Put the bundled egg into the 400-mL beaker. Add 2–3 heaping spoonsful of coffee grounds and enough water to cover the egg. If an empty eggshell is being used, a small beaker half-filled with water may be needed to weight down the bundled egg to keep it submerged. (See Figure B3.)

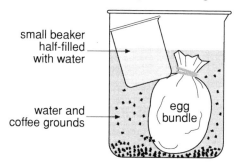

Figure B3: Weighting an eggshell in the dye bath

6. Place the beaker containing the egg bundle on a hot plate and boil gently for about 20 minutes.

7. Using a pair of tongs, remove the egg bundle and place it on several folded paper towels to cool.

8. Unwrap the bundle. Each Sassy Egg will be unique, with yellow from the onion skins, brown from the coffee, and white or colored shapes where the leaves and flowers were in contact with the egg.

9. (optional) Lightly coat the egg with vegetable oil to give it sheen and highlight the colors.

■ What's Sassy about Sassy Eggs?

Student Background 1: The Historical Importance of Natural Dyes

> When lovely woman tilts her saucer,
> And finds too late that tea will stain,
> Whatever made a Lady crosser,
> What act can wash all white again?
> The only art the stain to cover,
> To hide the spot from every eye
> And wear an unsoiled dress above her
> The proper color is to DYE.
>   —Joseph Swartz, "The Family Dyer"

No matter how seriously textile dyeing is discussed, it finally comes back to a simple but powerful basis: peoples' desire for beauty. The first western-European dyers were probably the Swiss Lake Dwellers who lived about 2000 B.C. In the East, Chinese writings mention dye workshops around 3000 B.C. Egyptian tombs at Thebes dating to 3500 B.C. contained indigo-dyed textiles. Egyptians of the 14th century B.C. understood the use of mordants (metallic salts that have an affinity for both fibers and dyestuffs) and the Phoenician dye industry in the 15th century B.C. was known for its purples obtained from a species of shellfish.

Trade in dyestuffs began as soon as the dye sources of one district were recognized as superior to those of another district. Indigo, from the *Indigofera* plant in India, was introduced to western Europe along the Phoenician trade routes when indigo was observed to give a deeper blue color than the traditionally used woad plant. Both plants actually contain the indigo dye but it is much less concentrated in the woad plant.

In the second half of the 12th century, Chretien de Troyes wrote of a traveling merchant in *Guillaume D'angleterre:*

> "Sire, my name is Guis from Galvaide
> From where I have a lot of madder and woad
> And brezil and alum and grain,
> With which I dye my linen and my wool."

Cochineal, a natural rich crimson dyestuff obtained from the insect *Dactylopius coccus*, was the first product to be exported from the New World to the Old. During the 16th century, Spanish explorers recognized the value of cochineal and reserved exclusive rights to sell it. French chemists using cochineal with tin as a mordant produced the bright scarlet for which the Gobelin tapestries of Paris became famous.

In colonial America, almost all professional dyers were trained in Europe, and imported dyes were the mainstay of their industry, though many individual dyers and home dyers extracted colors from local native plants. The American Indians, especially of the Southwest, were skilled in the use of plant dyes and used naturally occurring materials, such as raw alum and rock salt, as mordants.

Until the mid-19th century, dyers primarily used vegetable materials as the source of their dyestuffs. Leaves, roots, and barks furnished a somewhat narrow range of colors with limited variation in shades and tones. Raw materials varied considerably, so the results were somewhat unpredictable.

The year 1856 marked a turning point in the history of dyes. Sir William H. Perkin, while trying to synthesize the anti-malarial drug quinine from coal tar, accidentally produced the first synthetic dye, a purple color called mauve. Today nearly all dyes are produced synthetically. Synthetic dyes provide a wide range of color and reproducibility not found in dyes extracted from natural sources.

The latter half of the 20th century has seen a renewed interest in natural dyes. The revival of arts and crafts, interest in anything "natural," and environmental concerns sparked this interest. The unpredictability of results is another attractive feature of dyeing with natural materials; each dye bath provides a "one-of-a-kind" color.

■ What's Sassy About Sassy Eggs?

Overhead 1: The Dye Works

Courtesy of Smithsonian Institution, Division of Textiles

■ What Makes Dyes Work?

Student Background 2: Natural Dyes and Wool

Dyeing is a chemical process. For centuries, dyers recorded their attempts to understand the chemistry of the coloring materials they used. In 70 A.D. Pliny the Elder wrote:

> "…the white cloth being first stained in various places not with dyestuffs, but with drugs, which have the property of absorbing colors. These applications do not appear on the cloth, but when the cloths are afterwards plunged into a cauldron containing the dye liquor they are withdrawn fully dyed of several colors according to the different properties of the drugs which have been applied."

And in 1806, Elijah Bemiss wrote in "Dyer's Companion":

> "The five Material Colors are these, blue, yellow, red, brown and black; the three powers are these, the Alkali, the Acid and the Corrosive; these are the depending powers of all colors."

From Pliny through the centuries to Bemiss, dyes and mordants were classified as drugs. The druggist was interchangeably known as the chemist. Today we still turn to chemistry to understand dyes and the dyeing process.

Natural dyes are materials found in nature that have the capacity to impart color to fiber. Most of these materials are water soluble. When dyes dissolve in water, they may remain intact as neutral molecules or they may dissociate into charged particles called ions. The form in which the dye occurs in a water solution affects the way it interacts with fibers.

The Structure of Wool

Especially in the case of chemically bonded dyes, the chemistry of the fiber is as important as that of the dyestuff. Most natural dyes are used to dye fibers of animal origin.

In this monograph, we use wool as an example of an animal fiber which is commonly dyed with natural dyes. Wool consists of many long helical protein molecules called alpha-keratin, named for their alpha-helix shape (α-helix). This helical structure is held in place by hydrogen bonds between different parts of the chain. (See Figure B4.)

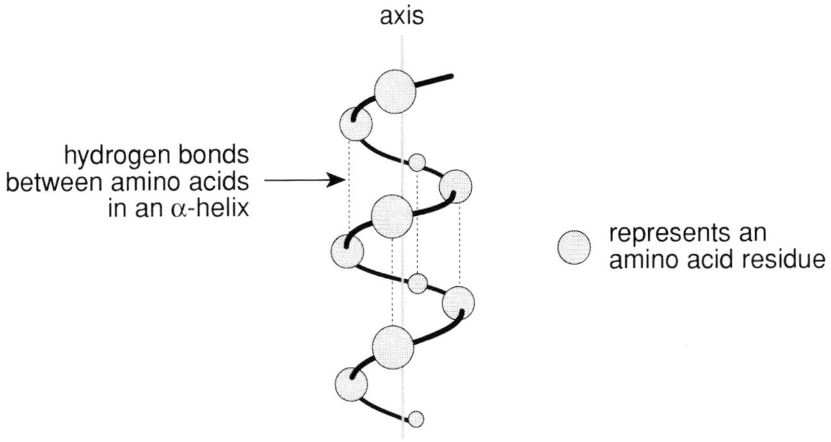

axis

hydrogen bonds
between amino acids
in an α-helix →

⬤ represents an
amino acid residue

Figure B4: Intramolecular hydrogen bonding holds the keratin in an α-helix orientation.

In keratin, several helical chains combine to form multichain cables. The protein chains making up these cables are held together by four important types of forces: hydrogen bonds, ionic bonds, disulfide bonds, and hydrophobic interactions. (See Figure B5.)

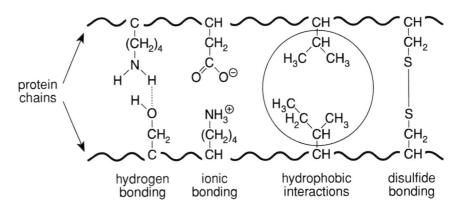

hydrogen
bonding   ionic
bonding   hydrophobic
interactions   disulfide
bonding

*Figure B5: Four types of forces are typically responsible
for holding the protein molecules in keratin together.*

Hydrogen bonding is a very important force in wool. In addition to being responsible for wool's basic helical structure (mentioned previously), hydrogen bonds also exist between the different protein side chains in the helix cables. Hydrogen bonding takes place between the hydrogen of an amine group ($-NH_2$) or hydroxyl group ($-OH$) from one amino acid residue and a carbonyl oxygen ($C=O$) amide on a neighboring amino acid residue.

Ionic bonds, known as salt bridges, are also present in wool. These form between a cation (+ charged) and an anion (– charged) on adjacent molecules.

Disulfide bonds, which provide the only covalent bonds between adjoining α-helixes, are formed when two cysteine units (whether on the same chain or on two different chains) are oxidized to form a single cystine unit. (See Figure B6.) In addition to adding strength to the fiber, the pattern of disulfide bonds influences and fixes the curliness of the fiber.

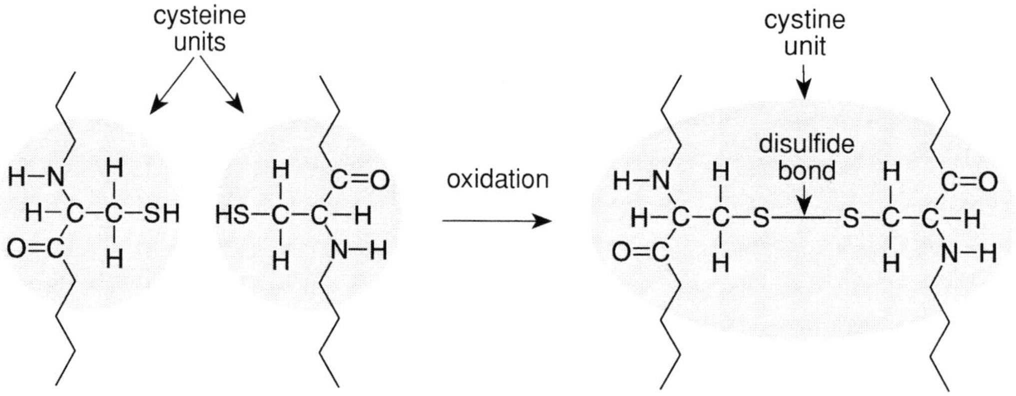

Figure B6: A disulfide bond is formed between two cysteine units.

While not involved in the dyeing process, the disulfide bridges can be affected by concentrated acids or bases. High concentrations of strong acids or bases can break the disulfide bonds and thus weaken the wool fiber as the cross-linking between protein chains is disrupted. Concentrated acids and bases also disrupt the hydrogen bonds and salt bridges.

The fourth type of interaction is called hydrophobic interaction. This is the weakest of the four types of forces and results when nonpolar groups interact to prevent water molecules from entering.

■ What Makes Dyes Work?

Overhead 2: Hydrogen Bonding in Keratin

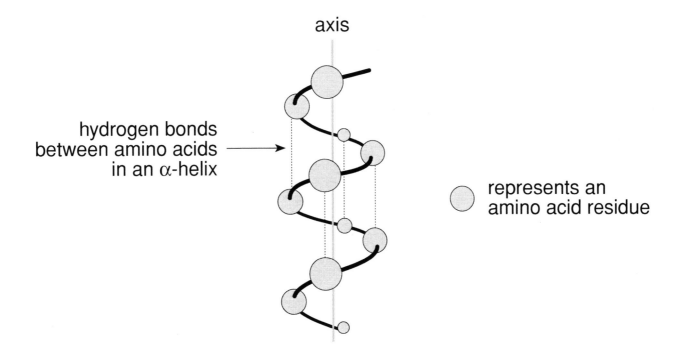

axis

hydrogen bonds
between amino acids
in an α-helix →

represents an
amino acid residue

What Makes Dyes Work?

Overhead 3: Four Types of Interactions or Forces in Keratin

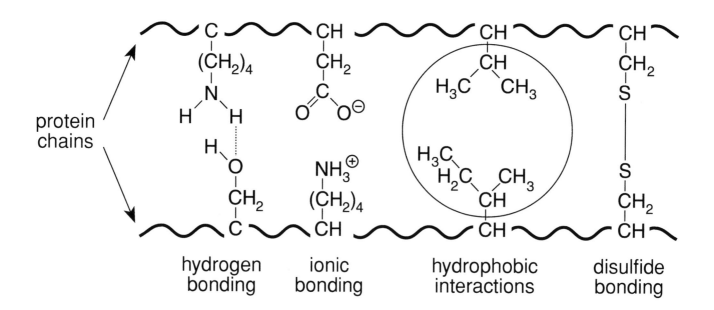

■ What Makes Dyes Work?

Overhead 4: Formation of a Cystine Unit from the Oxidation of Two Cysteine Units

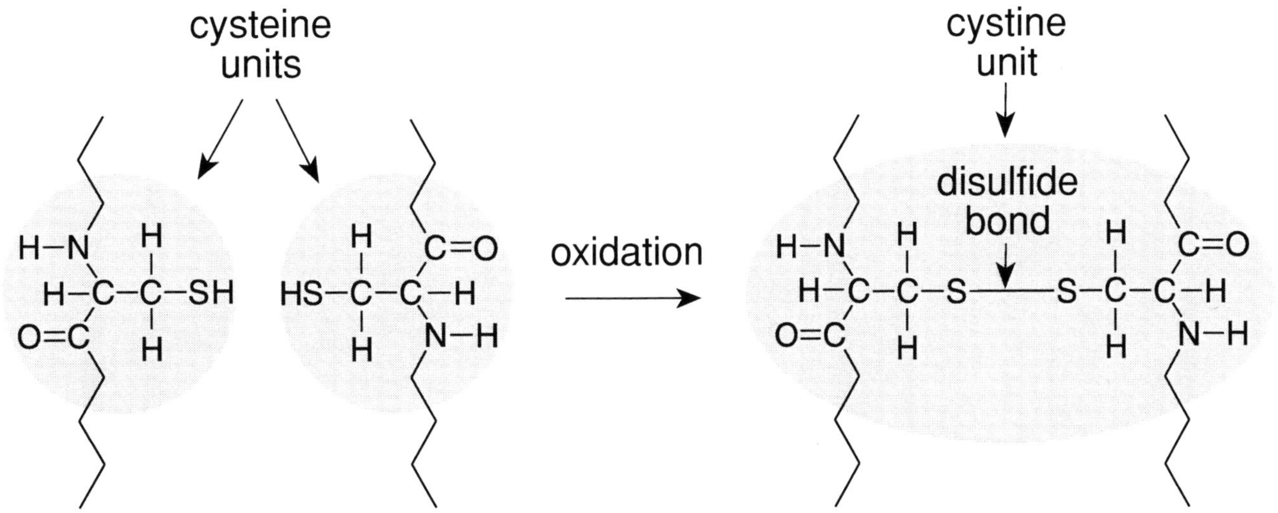

cysteine
units

cystine
unit

oxidation

disulfide
bond

◼ What's Your Favorite Color?

Student Background 3: Natural Sources of Important Colors

Any color, so long as it's red,
Is the color that suits me best,
Though I will allow there is much to be said
For yellow and green and the rest.
—Eugene Field, "Red"

Of the numerous natural dyes known, the majority are of vegetable origin, coming from plants, trees, and lichens. A few natural dyes are obtained from insects and mollusks.

Red

Rubia tinctorium

Of the major natural red dyes, madder *(Rubia tinctorium)* is the only one of vegetable origin. The others are derived from insects. During the 1400s the Dutch became proficient in the cultivation of madder and the extraction of its dye. The dye constituent of madder is alizarin. (See Figure B7.) In the madder plant, the bulk of the dye is contained in a red mass between the outer skin and the woody heart of the root.

Figure B7: Structure of alizarin

Tunics dyed in madder were used by armies of both France and England. The English "Redcoats" of the Revolutionary War derisively referred to the American forces as "blue-bellied Yankees," as the blue of their uniforms was considered a commonplace dye color.

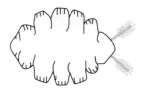

Dactylopius coccus

When Spanish explorers entered Mexico in 1518 they found the Aztec Indians dyeing with cochineal. This red dyestuff which the Spaniards initially mistook for seeds was actually the dried bodies of the insect *Dactylopius coccus* which lived on the Opuntia cactus. The coloring material in cochineal, carminic acid (See Figure B8), produces beautiful crimsons, scarlets, and pinks on wool and silk.

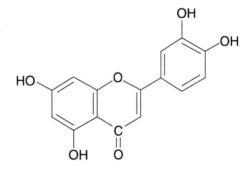

Figure B8: Structure of carminic acid

Approximately 70,000 dried insects are required to produce 1 pound of cochineal. Although high-priced, cochineal was a staple red dye during the 1800s.

Yellow

Reseda luteola

Plants which provide yellow dyes are abundant. A wide range of yellows, golds, and bronzes can be created from plants such as goldenrod, turmeric, and sassafras and from the wood or bark of trees such as white ash, hickory, peach, and Osage orange.

Weld *(Reseda luteola)* is of greater antiquity than any other yellow dye source. It was highly prized by the Romans, who restricted yellow to bridal garments. Weld was the most important dye of the Middle Ages and was widely cultivated in France, Italy, Germany, and England. In combination with the blue dye, woad, it produced Lincoln Green, made famous by Robin Hood and his merry men.

The entire weld plant, with exception of the roots, contains coloring matter. The seeds and the upper leaves are richest in the pigment. The chemical structure of its active dye, luteolin, is shown in Figure B9.

Figure B9: Structure of luteolin

Blue

Indigofera tinctoria

Indigo (See Figure B10), the dyestuff most widely used in America during the 18th and 19th centuries, is the blue dye responsible for the blue in "blue jeans." Its natural form is extracted from the leaves of the *Indigofera* plant, native to India. Only about 4 ounces of indigo can be extracted from 100 pounds of plant material and the preparation for its use as a dye requires many steps. Therefore, it is not surprising that synthetic indigo has now almost entirely replaced the natural product.

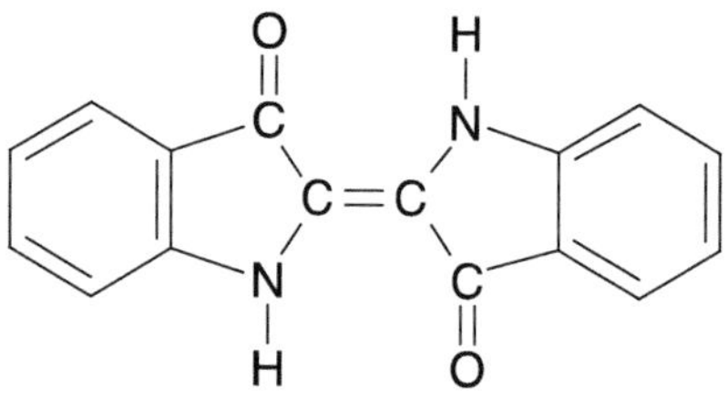

Figure B10: Structure of indigo

Prior to the introduction of indigo from India early in the 16th century, woad was the only blue dye used in Western Europe. It was the earliest plant to be cultivated specifically for its pigment. Throughout many centuries the use of woad was an important industry. Its dyers organized into guilds and the dyeing techniques were passed on from father to son. The dye component in both woad and the *Indigofera* plant is the structure shown in Figure B10. Indigo is much more concentrated in the *Indigofera* plant than it is in woad, and the introduction of indigo from the East, though fought successfully for many years by the dyers' guilds, gradually replaced woad and brought an end to the woad industry.

Indigo, along with other vat dyes, belongs to a class of dyes known as mechanically bonded dyes or precipitate dyes. These dyes do not react chemically with fiber. Vegetable fibers, such as cotton, are often dyed using vat dyes. In a vat dye, neutral molecules of the dye are precipitated within the fibers and mechanically trapped in place. While chemically bonded dyes make up the majority of natural dyes, vat dyes such as indigo have had a great deal of historical importance. The chemistry of vat dyes is covered in a separate monograph of the *Palette of Color* series, *The Chemistry of Vat Dyes.*

Purple

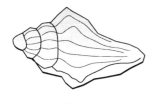

Murex

Tiny mollusk shells (genus *Murex*), found on the Phoenician coast near the city of Tyre, produce a beautiful purple. The coloring agent in Tyrian Purple is dibromindigo. (See Figure B11.)

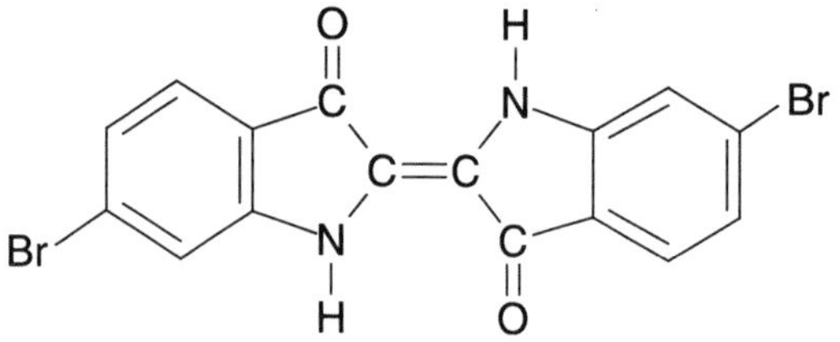

Figure B11: Structure of 6, 6'-dibromindigo

By 1500 B.C., Tyre had become the center for the trading and manufacture of purple dye. Tyrian purple was exceedingly costly to make because it took approximately 12,000 shells to produce 1 gram of the dyestuff. Because of its rare and costly nature, purple came to be closely associated with royalty. Purple sails powered Cleopatra's barge and Julius and Augustus Caesar both decreed that, in the Roman Empire, none but the emperor and his household might wear purple.

Black

Logwood *(Haematoxylon campechianum)* is the source of a deep black dye and is one of the few natural dyes which was used on a commercial scale well into the 20th century. The coloring agent in logwood is haematin. (See Figure B12.) Synthetic black dyes of good quality are hard to produce, so even today some logwood is used to dye leather.

Haematoxylon campechianum

Figure B12: Structure of haematin

Logwood was a product of the New World, native to Central America, Mexico, and many parts of South America. The logwood dye is obtained from the reddish heartwood of the *Haematoxylon campechianum* tree. Marketed in large blocks of up to 400 pounds, the wood is reduced to chips and fermented to extract the dye. This dye is only fast, or permanent, if appropriate mordants are used.

■ What's Your Favorite Color?

Overhead 5: A Madder Plant

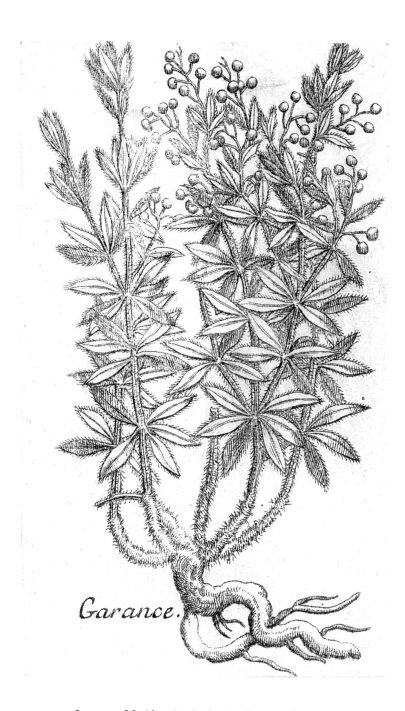

Garance.

Courtesy of Smithsonian Institution, Division of Textiles

■ What's Your Favorite Color?

Activity 2: What Color Will Appear?

Dyes are readily obtained from many plant materials. Natural dyestuffs produce subtle, one-of-a-kind colors. No two dye lots are identical, each having slight differences due to the growing conditions of the plant used or the impurities in the natural material. The color obtained from a plant may not be at all what one would predict. The outer dull brown of the madder root gives no clue to the bright red dye that lies within.

In this experiment you will extract the dye colors from several natural materials.

Safety

Eye protection should be worn during this experiment.

Materials

Per pair of students
- 6 250-mL beakers
- 400-mL beaker
- glass stirring rod
- beaker tongs
- 4 pieces of wool yarn each approximately 10 cm long
- hot plate
- green tops from 3 or 4 carrots
- yellow onion skins (about 150 mL dry)
- distilled water
- 4 zipper-type plastic bags
- masking tape and pen for labels
- 3 Red Zinger tea bags
- 4 chamomile tea bags
- goggles for each student

Procedure

1. Cut or tear carrot tops into pieces until you have 100–150 mL packed into a 250-mL beaker. Cover the carrot tops with distilled water and place the beaker on the hot plate.

2. Put the onion skins in a 250-mL beaker. Cover the onions skins with distilled water and place the beaker on the hot plate.

3. Put the 3 Red Zinger tea bags into 200 mL distilled water in a 250-mL beaker and place the beaker on the hot plate.

4. Put the 4 chamomile tea bags into 200 mL distilled water in a 250-mL beaker and place the beaker on the hot plate.

5. Simmer the liquids in the beakers for 30 minutes. (Do not boil hard.)

6. Remove the tea bags from the beakers.

7. Using beaker tongs to hold the hot beakers, decant the liquids from the carrot tops and onion skins into two clean 250-mL beakers.

8. Place one strand of yarn in each dye bath and heat gently for 15 minutes.

9. Fill the 400-mL beaker with warm tap water.

10. Using the glass stirring rod, remove the yarn pieces from the dye baths and rinse each thoroughly in the warm water.

11. Lay the samples on a paper towel to dry.

12. When the yarn samples are dry, place them in labeled zipper-type plastic bags and complete the following data table.

Results of Activity 2	
Dye Material	Color of Dyed Wool
carrot tops	
onion skins	
Red Zinger	
chamomile	

Summary Questions

1. Were the colors of the dye baths the same as the colors of the original natural materials?

2. Were the colors of the dyed yarn samples the same as the colors of the dye baths?

3. Which dye seemed to give the most intense color to the yarn sample?

4. Which dye appeared to "wash out" of the yarn sample the most?

■ Can We Change a Dye's Color?

Activity 3: How Is Dye Color pH-Dependent?

Chemically bonded dyes undergo a chemical reaction with the fiber. Simple or substantive dyes bond directly to wool at a salt bridge. One type of substantive dyes is known as acid dyes. Acid dyes contain an acid functional group such as $-SO_3H$ or $-COOH$. These dyes ionize in water, yielding dye fragments which are negatively charged ions. (See Figure B13.)

$$dye-(SO_3H)_n \ + \ H_2O \longrightarrow dye-(SO_3^{\ominus})_n \ + \ H_3O^{\oplus}$$

Figure B13: Ionization of an acid dye

These negatively charged ions bond to cationic sites on the fiber, such as the $-NH_3^+$ group on the polypeptide chain in wool. The negative ions of an acid dye are attracted to a positively charged site of the wool (for example, NH_3^+) and retained on the fiber due to ionic bonding. These negative and positive dye ions form salt bridges between the fiber and the dye. (See Figure B14.)

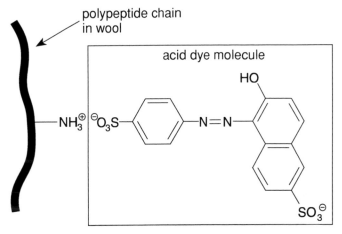

Figure B14: Ionic bonding of dye molecule to wool

The bonding of dyes to fibers is often pH-dependent. In an acidic dye bath, more of the basic amino groups ($-NH_2$) on the wool are protonated to form $-NH_3^+$. This allows attraction of more anionic functional groups. Conversely, under basic conditions, few amino groups are protonated; thus fewer cationic sites are available for bonding to the acid dyes.

In this experiment, you will observe the effect of changing pH on the colors of two natural dyes.

Safety

Eye protection should be worn for this experiment; ammonia and its vapors can damage the eyes. Do not wear contact lenses when working with ammonia because gaseous vapors may condense on the contact lens and damage the eye.

Use ammonia only in a well-ventilated area. Should contact with the eyes occur, rinse the affected area with water for 15 minutes and seek medical attention while rinsing is occurring.

Materials

Per pair of students
- 3 250-mL beakers
- 6 150-mL beakers
- glass stirring rod
- beaker tongs
- 4 Hydrion paper strips
- 6 pieces of wool yarn each approximately 10 cm long
- 6 zipper-type plastic bags
- green tops from 3 or 4 carrots
- yellow onion skins (about 150 mL dry)
- about 3 mL vinegar
- about 3 mL 1 M ammonia solution
- hot plate
- distilled water
- goggles for each student

Procedure

1. Cut or tear carrot tops into pieces until you have 100–150 mL packed into a 250-mL beaker. Cover the carrot tops with distilled water and place the beaker on the hot plate.

2. Put the onion skins in a 250-mL beaker. Cover the onion skins with distilled water and place the beaker on the hot plate.

3. Simmer the liquids in the beakers for 30 minutes. (Do not boil hard.)

4. Using beaker tongs to hold the hot beakers, decant the liquid from the carrot tops into three 150-mL beakers and number the beakers 1–3.

5. Repeat Step 4, pouring the liquid from the onion skins into a second set of three beakers.

6. Using Hydrion paper, adjust the pH to 3–4 in the number 1 beakers by the addition of vinegar.

7. Using Hydrion paper, adjust the pH to 10 in the number 3 beakers by the addition of 1 M ammonia solution.

8. Using Hydrion paper, determine the pHs of the solutions in the number 2 beakers and record on the data table. (The solutions in the number 2 beakers should remain unchanged; add nothing.)

9. Place one piece of yarn in each beaker and heat all six beakers gently for 15 minutes.

10. Fill a 250-mL beaker two-thirds full of warm tap water.

11. Using the glass stirring rod, remove the yarn from each dye bath. Rinse the samples thoroughly in the warm water and lay them on a paper towel to dry.

12. When the samples are dry, place them in labeled zipper-type plastic bags and complete the data table.

Results of Activity 3			
Beaker Number	Dye Material	pH	Color of Dyed Wool
1	carrot tops	3–4	
2	carrot tops		
3	carrot tops	10	
1	onion skins	3–4	
2	onion skins		
3	onion skins	10	

Summary Questions

1. Ammonia is a weak base. Why would it be inadvisable to use a strong base such as sodium hydroxide for this procedure?

2. Soap solutions are often very basic in character. What would the effect be of rinsing the acid-dyed wool in a soapy solution?

■ Can We Change a Dye's Color?

Overhead 6: Ionic Bonding Between Anionic Dye and Cationic Site on the Protein Fiber

polypeptide chain
in wool

acid dye molecule

■ Can We Change a Dye's Color?

Student Background 4: Mordants

A common problem with natural dyes is their "fugitive" behavior. While initially providing a pleasing color, the color "flees" from the fabric upon exposure to light or repeated washing. Early in dyeing history, it was discovered that if certain metallic salts were added to wool, the dyeings became very wash-fast. These metal salts were called mordants (from the French word, "mordre," "to bite"). It was thought that these salts helped the dye bite into the wool and hold it fast during washings.

Aluminum ion (Al^{3+}), chromium(III) ion (Cr^{3+}), copper(II) ion (Cu^{2+}), iron(III) ion (Fe^{3+}), and tin(II) ion (Sn^{2+}) are commonly used as mordants. Figure B15 provides a generalized equation showing how a chromium(III) ion could react to form a bridge between the dye molecule and the protein fiber.

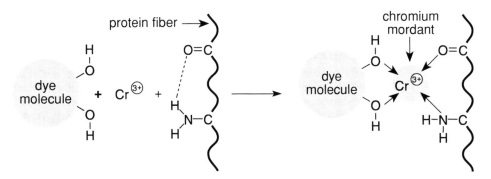

Figure B15: A mordant bridge between a dye molecule and the fiber

Generally, the wool is pre-treated with a solution of the metal salt in order to allow the metal ions to attach themselves to the wool before dyeing. When the dye is introduced, it forms an insoluble complex salt, sometimes called a lake, with the metal ion within the fiber. This large, complex molecule is less water soluble than the individual dye molecules so possesses greater wet-fastness. Mordants are also used to increase the range of colors available from a given dye. One of the natural dyes with the greatest reported range of colors is logwood. Depending on the mordants used and the application processes, logwood can produce reds, purples, blues, grays, and blacks.

Many common materials are used as mordants. Household alum, $AlNH_4(SO_4)_2$ or $KAl(SO_4)_2$, and cream of tartar ($KHC_4H_4O_6$) are two of the most common. The use of alum as a mordant in Roman times is documented in Pliny's "Natural History" of 70 A.D. Cream of tartar is formed in the fermentation process of wine-making and was, at one time, obtained for use as a mordant by scraping the inside of wine casks.

Lacking the necessary chemicals for mordanting, dyers sometimes use the dye pot itself as a source of the metal ions. A tin pot will result in bright, sharp colors, while a copper pot will impart a green tone to dye colors.

■ Can We Change a Dye's Color?

Activity 4: How Do Mordants Affect Dye Colors?

A mordant acts as a chemical bridge between the dye molecule and the fiber. The mordant is usually a metal ion which attaches to both the dye and the fiber and forms a link between them. In this experiment you will study the effect of several mordants on natural dyes.

Safety

Eye protection should be worn for this experiment.

Materials

Per group of 4 students
- 4 250-mL beakers
- 4 100-mL beakers
- 2 glass stirring rods
- 16 pieces of wool yarn (each about 10 cm long)
- 2 hot plates
- beaker tongs
- yellow onion skins (about 150 mL dry)
- green tops from 3–4 carrots
- 3 Red Zinger tea bags
- 4 chamomile tea bags
- 1.5 g copper sulfate pentahydrate ($CuSO_4 \bullet 5H_2O$)
- 1.5 g alum, $AlNH_4(SO_4)_2$ or $KAl(SO_4)_2$
- 2.75 g cream of tartar
- 0.35 g tin(II) chloride ($SnCl_2$)
- distilled water
- goggles for each student

Procedure

1. Using the four 250-mL beakers, prepare the following dye baths:
   - dye bath 1: onion skins covered with distilled water;
   - dye bath 2: carrot tops torn into pieces and covered with distilled water;
   - dye bath 3: Red Zinger tea bags in 200 mL distilled water; and
   - dye bath 4: chamomile tea bags in 200 mL distilled water.

2. Place the four beakers on a hot plate and simmer the liquids in the beakers for 30 minutes. (Do not boil hard.)

3. Meanwhile, prepare the mordant solutions in three 100-mL beakers. (The fourth 100-mL beaker will contain distilled water.)
   - Beaker 1: Dissolve 1.5 g copper sulfate pentahydrate ($CuSO_4 \bullet 5H_2O$) in 75 mL distilled water.
   - Beaker 2: Dissolve 1.5 g alum and 0.75 g cream of tartar in 75 mL distilled water.
   - Beaker 3: Dissolve 0.35 g tin(II) chloride ($SnCl_2$) and 2.00 g cream of tartar in 75 mL distilled water.

4. Knot the samples of yarn according to the following code (Each mordant beaker will contain four pieces of yarn):
   - Beaker 1: copper mordant—knot in one end of yarn
   - Beaker 2: alum mordant—knot in both ends of yarn
   - Beaker 3: tin mordant—knot in center of yarn
   - Beaker 4: no mordant—no knot in yarn

5. Add four correspondingly knotted pieces of yarn to each mordant bath.

6. Place these beakers on a hot plate and simmer GENTLY for 30 minutes.

7. Using the glass stirring rod, remove the yarn from the mordant baths.

8. Lay the yarn aside on a paper towel.

9. Pour the mordant solutions down the drain (or save as directed by your teacher). Wash the beakers and rinse with distilled water.

10. Using the beaker tongs, decant approximately 75 mL of solution from dye bath 1 into beaker 1, 75 mL of solution from dye bath 2 into beaker 2, 75 mL of solution from dye bath 3 into beaker 3 and 75 mL from dye bath 4 into beaker 4. Discard the remaining dye solutions.

11. Place one piece of yarn from each mordant bath into each dye bath.

12. Simmer the yarn in the dye baths for 15 minutes, stirring occasionally.

13. Half-fill one of the 250-mL beakers with warm water.

14. Remove the yarn pieces from the dye baths, rinse them in the warm water, and lay them by coded groups on a paper towel to dry.

15. When the samples are dry, complete the following data table. Retain the samples for use in Activity 5.

Results of Activity 4		
Dye Material	Mordant	Color
carrot tops	copper	
	alum	
	tin	
	no mordant	
onion skins	copper	
	alum	
	tin	
	no mordant	
Red Zinger	copper	
	alum	
	tin	
	no mordant	
chamomile	copper	
	alum	
	tin	
	no mordant	

Summary Questions

1. Did each mordant affect the yarn in the same way?

2. Which mordant appeared to cause the most dramatic change in dye color?

3. Feel the dried yarn samples. Is there a difference in the way they feel? Why would one of the mordants perhaps be less desirable for wool?

4. Which mordant appeared to cause the least change in the dye color?

Can We Change a Dye's Color?

Overhead 7: The Mordant Chromium Ion Provides a Link Between the Dye Molecule and the Protein Fiber

■ Will the Dye Color Fade?

Student Background 5: Fast or Fugitive?

Standardized scientific tests for colorfastness are a relatively recent development in the dye industry, but concern with a dye's ability to retain its color is not new. Fastness has long been the mark of a useful dye. As early as the 1st century A.D., Plutarch commented on the lasting qualities of Tyrian Purple. It is said that the reason the American flag is red, white, and blue is that madder (red) and indigo (blue) were reliable, fast dyes, and natural white yarn was always available.

The difficulty with most natural dyes was that they lacked colorfastness. Thus, those dyes which *were* colorfast, such as indigo, became important trade items. Other dyes, such as logwood, only became commercially important when a mordant was found which would render them colorfast.

In medieval times, dyers were classed as either "dyers of fast colors" or "dyers of fugitive colors." Clients of the 18th and 19th centuries demanded high standards of colorfastness. One incident is recorded of an English dealer being forced to repay a buyer of dress calico because it faded after two years.

Impetus for modern colorfast studies came in 1901 or 1902 when James Morton, a famous Scottish textile maker, observed some of his own firm's tapestries in a shop window. Their faded condition horrified him, and when he learned they had only been on display for a week he resolved to produce a line of colorfast dyes. By 1906 the Morton Sandour Fabrics Ltd. advertised the first unfading fabrics carrying a guarantee "to resupply any goods found unsatisfactory in regards to fastness."

In 1948, the International Standards Organization (ISO) formed a "colorfastness subcommittee" which devised 50–60 standardized tests, including colorfastness to agents and actions encountered during *manufacture*, such as bleaching, sizing, chlorination, pleating, and colorfastness to agents encountered during *use*, such as artificial light, dry-cleaning, washing, and perspiration. Methods of testing, procedures, and standards are all detailed by the ISO.

The need for fastness in a dye varies with the use of the article to be dyed. The dye for printing paper napkins need not be as fast as the dye used for curtains or carpets. No dye is absolutely fast under all conditions. It may be fast to light but less fast to washing. Or, a dye may be fast on one fiber but not on another. Of all textile fibers, wool is the most easily dyed and the resulting color will change the least.

■ Will the Dye Color Fade?

Activity 5: How Colorfast Are Natural Dyes?

A successful dye must satisfy many conditions and one of the most important is colorfastness. One would not want to buy a dyed product if it would fade within several weeks. Considerable work has gone into the study of the fading process and all dye manufacturers carry out tests for the colorfastness of their dyes. In this experiment you will test the yarn samples you dyed in Activity 4 for colorfastness.

Safety

No special safety procedures are required for this experiment.

Materials

Per group of 4 students
- sheet of uncorrugated cardboard (The back of a tablet will work well.)
- duct tape or black plastic tape
- transparent tape
- yarn samples from Activity 4

Procedure

1. Fold up the bottom third of the cardboard sheet to make an envelope. (See Figure B16.)

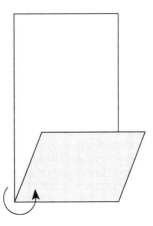

Figure B16: Cardboard envelope

2. Open the sheet and tape (with transparent tape) the 16 yarn samples on the upper portion. (See Figure B17.) The positions should be such that half of each sample is covered when the bottom flap is folded up. Number and record the position and nature of each sample (dye and mordant).

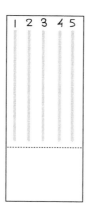

Figure B17: Placement of yarn samples in envelope

3. Refold the envelope so that the bottom half of the samples are between the cardboard layers. Tape it tightly with black duct tape. (See Figure B18.)

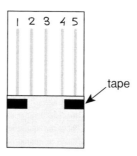

Figure B18: Taped envelope with yarn samples

4. Expose the yarn samples to direct sunlight over a period of six weeks.

5. Open the envelope and compare the color of the upper portion of the yarn, which was exposed to light, with the color of the lower portion, which was protected from the light by the taped envelope.

Summary Questions

1. Describe the results of your colorfastness tests.

2. Which of your natural dyes appeared to be "fast" and which appeared to be "fugitive"?

3. How did the use of mordants affect the colorfastness of the dyes?